Revamping Fashion Industry with Virtual Reality

Reality

The 3D Experience

Table of Contents

Chapter 1. Introduction

Discover a vibrant universe where innovation redefines tradition, introducing "Revamping Fashion Industry with Virtual Reality: The 3D Experience." This Special Report delves into how Virtual Reality (VR) plays a pivotal role in reshaping the fashion industry, adding another dimension to the way we view and engage with style. Embark on this exciting journey as we unravel the fusion between technology and fashion, uncover the way VR is transforming design processes, retail experiences, and even runway shows into immersive stories! From globe-trotting fashion enthusiasts to budding designers and tech enthusiasts, everyone has something to gain. Intriguing, insightful, and exhilarating, this Special Report not only uncovers the future of fashion but urges you to be an active participant in it! So, why just read about the future when you can experience it? Get your copy now and step into the exciting world where creativity meets technology.

Chapter 2. The Advent of Virtual Reality in Fashion

There's a transformation in the air; a change on the horizon which is going to fundamentally shift the very fabric of the fashion industry. Welcome to a world where Virtual Reality (VR), an immersive, multisensory technology, is set to revolutionize what we know about fashion - how we design it, how we sell it and indeed, how we perceive it. This chapter dives deep into the beginnings of this fusion between fashion and VR, the reasons behind it, and the contours of change we are beginning to see.

2.1. The Genesis of VR and Fashion

The birth of VR technology dates back to the 1950's with the development of flight simulators, but the idea of VR in fashion is a truly modern concept. As digitization began taking over various industries in the late 2000s, two distinct realms - fashion, a bastion of human creativity and expression, and technology, a testament to human innovation and progress - began to converge. This was the beginning of a symbiotic relationship between fashion and VR, just waiting to be explored.

2.2. Why VR Makes Sense for Fashion

By its very nature, fashion is a visual and tactile field. It's about more than just the clothes we wear - it's about the story behind each piece, the way it makes us feel, and the message it sends to the world about who we are. In this context, VR presents a unique opportunity. By creating an immersive, 3D environment, VR offers the prospect of a more holistic shopping experience; one where customers can virtually try on clothes, engage with them in a simulated space, and get a feel for the product that far exceeds the flat, 2D images of the traditional online shopping experience.

2.3. VR in Fashion Design

One of the first areas where VR has started to significantly impact fashion is in the realm of design. VR software, such as Clo3D and Tukatech, allow designers to create 3D models of their creations, applying textures and colors, and making changes on the fly. Not only does this rapidly accelerate the design process, it also allows designers to experiment in ways they never could before. Prototypes can be created and modified virtually, eliminating the need for expensive physical models, and entire collections can be designed and viewed in a three-dimensional space without ever touching a piece of fabric.

2.4. VR in Retail: Reinventing Shopping Experience

The potential of VR in retail is truly transformative. Imagine browsing a virtual mall from the comfort of your couch, or stepping into a VR dressing room to try on a dress and see how it would look on you from all angles, without ever leaving your house. This new level of immersive shopping made possible by VR is poised to redefine our concept of e-commerce. Companies like Tommy Hilfiger, Rebecca Minkoff, and ASOS have already started to exploit this potential, adopting VR to create unique and highly individualized shopping experiences.

2.5. Runway Shows: From Physical to Virtual

Even runway shows, the physical embodiment of the high-octane glamour of the fashion industry, haven't been immune to the VR revolution. In a world before VR, fashion shows were an exclusive event with limited audience. Fast-forward to now, and we have brands like Moschino and Balenciaga creating full-on virtual reality shows, open to everyone and anyone with a headset. These shows allow for a completely new experience, where the viewer can even be on the runway alongside models and experience the show from an insider's point of view.

2.6. VR: The Future is Here

The implications of VR in the fashion industry are not just limited to the present. For budding designers, VR technology can offer a new medium for showcasing creativity and expanding their portfolio. Retailers can employ VR tech to enhance customer shopping experiences and ultimately improve overall satisfaction and loyalty. And for consumers, VR in fashion provides a novel approach to explore, experience, and engage with fashion in ways we couldn't even imagine before.

The pace at which the fusion between VR and fashion is taking place suggests a vibrant future, rife with immersive storytelling, experiential retail, and broadly inclusive fashion shows. What started as two parallel paths in the vast woods of human endeavor has intersected in spectacular fashion, altering the course of both. VR is much more than merely a tool in fashion; it is the pulse of a new dimension, heralding an era where innovation is not just about tradition but about surpassing it. The advent of VR in fashion is more than just a technological breakthrough - it's a cultural shift, a new paradigm, and most importantly, it is only just beginning.

As we delve deeper into this topic, we will further explore how VR is paving unique paths within the fashion industry, drilling into specifics of these transformations and their implications on designers, retailers, and consumers alike. From design inception to consumer engagement, we will journey through this virtual revolution in fashion. Acquainting ourselves with immersive technology and the fashion industry's adoption of the same will enlighten us regarding the future of this symbiosis - one that promises to be as vibrant and exciting as it is transformative.

Here is a promise for a journey that is not just about discovery, but about participating and engaging in seismic shifts in industry and culture. Welcome to the future of fashion, where style meets the refined power of technology, to create regal strides in the industry, and the world. And remember, this isn't just a narrative you're reading - this is a narrative you're becoming part of.

Chapter 3. Re-imagining Design Processes with VR

In the vibrant milieu of the fashion industry, Virtual Reality (VR) is emerging as a revolutionary tool that's drastically changing the current design processes. By introducing a third dimension and a scope for realistic virtual interaction, VR provides a new lens to designers, creating an environment where innovation thrives and possibility is the only constant.

3.1. The New Canvas

In the world of VR, constraints are far fewer. Designers are no longer confined to the flat, 2D space of pen and paper or computer screens. Instead, they're free to work in three dimensions, replicating the physical properties of real-world materials and the draping of actual fabrics with precision and without wastage. They can design, edit, and view a line of clothing in real time, in a free-flowing, iterative process that increases creativity and effectiveness.

3.2. Testing and Iterations

Virtual prototypes created in VR environments are more than just digital approximations, they are close to the real-life representations of the intended outfits. Designers can swiftly make changes, viewing adjustments to the garment immediately rather than waiting for a physical sample. This system cuts down on the repetitive cycle of create-review-edit, saving time, labor, and material.

3.3. Immersive Showcasing

For designers, presenting their creations in VR means more than just displaying their work – it's about storytelling and providing an immersive experience. Unlike traditional design programs, VR allows the viewer to 'enter' the design space, to become a part of the environment and experience the design from within. This paves the way for memorable and compelling visual presentations that traditional mediums simply can't match.

3.4. Real-time Collaboration

Collaboration is crucial in the fashion industry. With VR, designers are better able to convey their ideas to their teams, cutting through the loss that occurs when translating a 2D design into a 3D product. By creating and visualizing in the same medium where the final piece will exist, misunderstandings and misinterpretations can be eliminated.

3.5. Sustainable Practices

Fostering sustainability is a major challenge for the global fashion industry. Fortunately, VR can encourage eco-friendly practices. By creating virtual prototypes, designers eliminate the need for physical samples, contributing significantly to waste reduction. Additionally, virtual 'fitting rooms' can minimize the volume of returns and unsold inventory.

3.6. The Customer Connection

In the end, everything circles back to the consumer. VR can enhance the customer-designer connection, offering the customer a deeper understanding of the creative process. It allows the designer to tell the story of their creation, transporting the customer directly into the designer's studio and granting them an exclusive behind-the-scenes look at how the garments are brought to life.

Virtual Reality does more than just enhance the tools available to designers. It reinvents their workspace, transforming how they interact with their material, how they visualize their creations, how they communicate their ideas, and how they present their final pieces. It's this transformative potential that promises to define the future of the fashion industry - a future that's more efficient, more inclusive, more sustainable, and ultimately more creatively satisfying.

As we move deeper into this future, the intersection of VR and fashion design continues to be a space to watch, a frontier that brings the promise of unimagined design possibilities. With the adoption of VR, the traditional designing process is reinvented, making way for a more innovative and immersive fashion realm. Indeed, it's not just about changing realities; it's about creating new ones.

So with the advantage of this groundbreaking virtual technology, let's step boldly into the world of tomorrow, demonstrating that the future of fashion rests not just in following the trends, but in being the ones to set them. Virtual reality is an invitation to every designer to write their own future, to take the lead in shaping the next big thing in fashion, and to be the change we all anticipate. With VR, the future is truly now.

Chapter 4. 3D Modeling and Prototyping: Visualizing Ideas

In the contemporary fashion industry, the ability to visualize ideas in a tangible manner before their material production can be a game-changer. This capability allows designers to test, modify, and perfect their designs in a virtual environment, leading to fewer resource inputs and a more effective design process. Herein, 3D modeling and prototyping have revolutionized the fashion landscape, enabling designers to bring their creative dreams into (virtual) reality.

4.1. The Basics of 3D Modeling

3D modeling refers to the creation of a mathematical representation of a three-dimensional object utilizing specialized software. Its application in the fashion industry has been transformative, providing designers with a versatile tool to craft, modify, and refine their designs digitally.

Models are sculpted digitally within the virtual canvas of the software, similar to how clay would be moulded in an artist's hands. The software provides the capability to manipulate numerous factors, including color, texture, and shape. With these tools in hand, fashion designers are able to generate a virtual replica of their designs, which can be viewed from multiple angles and in different environments.

4.2. How 3D Prototyping is Changing Fashion Design

After 3D models are complete, they can be virtually prototyped, a stage crucial to the pre-production process. Prototyping brings designs to life, allowing them to be adjusted, tweaked, or completely redesigned before any physical manufacturing begins.

Virtual prototypes can display a design's movement, drape, and feel - components traditionally challenging to capture in 2D sketches. Particularly, in the case of intricate designs involving complex embellishments or layered materials, 3D prototyping offers a level of visual information that simply cannot be achieved through traditional methods.

4.3. The Role of Software in Rendering 3D Models

Software solutions are integral to the 3D modeling and prototyping process. This includes both design-specific software and more general 3D modeling programs.

Design-specific software, such as CLO, Optitex, and Browzwear, allows designers to work with virtual mannequins that can be customized to any body type. This ensures that designs are inclusive, adaptable, and well-fitted to diverse body forms, a versatile feature that's difficult to achieve with traditional mannequins.

On the other hand, general 3D modeling software such as Blender, Maya, and 3DS Max offers detailed design tools that allow for the creation of complex and unique details in your fashion designs.

4.4. Integrating VR into 3D Modeling and Prototyping

One of the most exciting developments in the digital fashion sphere is the integration of Virtual Reality (VR) into 3D modeling and prototyping processes. VR, known for its immersive capabilities, adds another dimension to the visualization process. Designers can 'step into' their creations, experiencing them in a fully immersive, realistic, and interactive environment.

In fact, VR can take prototyping to a new level. With VR, designers are no longer limited to observing their 3D models on a screen but can experience their creations in their intended state – on a virtual avatar in a simulated environment.

4.5. Future-forward: The Road Ahead for 3D Modeling and Prototyping

In the midst of digital transformation, the future of 3D modeling and prototyping in the fashion industry appears bright. As technology develops and becomes more affordable, it's likely that we will see wider usage and even more innovative applications.

Digital runway shows, for example, could eventually become the norm; designers might not just conceptualize and create their designs through 3D modeling and prototyping, but also showcase them to the world in cinematically rendered, virtually immersive fashion shows.

In conclusion, 3D modeling and prototyping are indeed redefining the fashion arena, pushing boundaries and urging us to reimagine the limits of design. As we stand on the brink of this exciting new era, one thing is clear: the fusion of fashion with technology is the pathway to the industry's future.

Chapter 5. Interactive Retail: Revolutionizing the Shopping Experience

Today, the global retail landscape, after being relatively static for decades, is evolving at a brisk pace. The rapid advent of digital technologies coupled with their increased accessibility has triggered this dynamic shift. At the heart of this transformation stands Virtual Reality (VR), revolutionizing the retail sector and redefining the way we shop. The use of VR in retail, particularly the fashion industry, presents a plethora of opportunities for unprecedented customer engagement and enriched shopping experiences.

5.1. Embracing the Virtual Shopping Trend

Presently, one of the most dominant trends in e-commerce is virtual shopping. Customers are no longer satisfied with static images of products on an e-commerce website. They seek an immersive experience that brings them as close as possible to physically seeing and trying on the clothes. Enter Virtual Reality. With VR, customers can now navigate through a virtual store just as they would in a physical one. They can look at products from multiple angles, view them in different lights, and even virtually try them on. This experience, no doubt, positively influences purchasing decisions, as customers can make more informed choices about what they buy.

5.2. Transforming Fitting Rooms

One of the persistent issues with online shopping has been the inability to try clothes on before purchasing. VR comes to the rescue, offering virtual fitting rooms. These rooms use customer-specific measurements to provide an accurate representation of how garments will look and fit on the individual. This VR try-on technology significantly reduces product returns, a problem that plagues the online fashion industry, and enhances customer satisfaction, since customers have a more realistic idea of what they are buying.

5.3. Redefining Consumer Engagement

Utilizing VR doesn't just involve replicating the physical shopping experience in a digital domain; it involves enhancing it. VR opens up a world of opportunities to engage consumers in innovative ways. Fashion retailers can use VR to deliver personalized content to customers, enhancing their experience and fostering brand loyalty. From curated fashion shows to wardrobe recommendations based on an individual's preferences and body type, VR has the potential to take consumer engagement to a new level.

5.4. Revamping Store Layouts and Visual Merchandising

VR isn't only beneficial for customers but for retailers as well. VR technology enables retailers to experiment with different store layouts and visual merchandising without investing time, effort, and money into physically executing them. They can analyze how these elements influence customer behavior and make data-driven decisions to optimize their store, ultimately improving sales and customer experience.

5.5. Bringing the Runway to Customers' Living Rooms

Fashion seasons usually bring the excitement of runway shows, the joy of exploring new trends, and the adrenalin rush of seeing models strut down the runway in stunning outfits. However, not everyone has the privilege of attending these shows. Here, again, VR steps in. Fashion houses and retailers can now bring their runway shows to customers' living rooms. Using VR headsets, customers can enjoy a 360-degree view of the catwalk, focusing on the outfits they like and examining them in fine detail. This immersive experience not only builds customer enthusiasm but also allows immediate purchase, streamlining the journey from runway to wardrobe.

5.6. The Future of Virtual Reality in Retail

The incorporation of VR in retail, specifically fashion, is still in its relative infancy, and many advancements are expected in the future. From increasingly realistic haptic feedback to hyper-personalized virtual shopping assistants, the possibilities are endless. As technology continues to develop, the quality, fidelity, and depth of VR experiences will only improve.

The fusion of VR and retail is more than a trendy innovation. It pioneers an immersive, interactive, and personalized shopping journey that takes customer experience to an unprecedented level. As we stride forward, it is exciting to think not just about the opportunities that VR technology provides today, but also about the potential it holds in revolutionizing retail.

With big names in the fashion industry already harnessing the power of VR, it is inevitable that VR will influence every aspect of the fashion retail process, pushing the boundaries of traditional shopping methods. Embracing this technology can give fashion brands a competitive edge over others and help them shape the future of retail.

In conclusion, VR holds the promise of transforming the retail landscape, weaving the convenience and infinite inventory of online shopping with the immersive and personal engagement of brick-and-mortar shopping. As we venture deeper into the world of VR and retail, it's thrilling to envision how this interaction will unfold. The most forward-thinking fashion brands will anticipate this trend moving even further ahead, adopting innovative ways to meld virtual reality into customers' shopping experiences.

Chapter 6. Runway Revolution: Virtual Fashion Shows

With the rise of virtual reality, the traditional world of fashion runways is undergoing a massive revolution. This pivotal transformation sees the fashion industry and VR technology blending seamlessly, revolutionizing our perception of fashion, and reshaping it to align with the digital world we inhabit today.

6.1. Turning to Tech: Rise of Virtual Runways

For years, runways have been the go-to means for designers to showcase their creativity and latest fashion statements. These glamorous events orchestrating a stunning spectacle of art, creativity, and style, set fashion trends that consumers follow worldwide. However, as the world became more global and digitalized, challenges around accessibility, sustainability, and inclusivity began to question these traditional fashion shows' relevance.

The answer lies in the robust embrace of virtual reality in the fashion world. This adoption has seen the dawn of virtual runways— an exciting alternative offering immersive experiences to stakeholders globally. The first major stride towards this was seen in 2020 when Shanghai Fashion Week went fully digital due to pandemic restrictions, reaching millions of online viewers globally in unprecedented ways and affirming the potential VR holds in transforming fashion shows.

Virtual runways allow designers to showcase their collections creatively through immersive experience-led storytelling. This not only enhances the overall presentation but also maintains the emotional connection between the designs and viewers previously felt only in an actual show.

6.2. Creating the Digital Design: From Sketch to 3D Models

Creating virtual fashion shows starts with transforming the sketches and swatches into digital designs using 3D modeling techniques. High-precision scanners capture every detail and texture of fabrics and then integrate them with digital frameworks that replicate the drape and flow of material.

Once the digital designs are complete, these are brought to life through 3D animation showing movement and interaction within the virtual environment. This step is crucial to adding the show's depth and dimension replicating the look and feel of live models walking on a runway.

6.3. Runway in Your Room: Immersive Experiences at Home

Hosting virtual fashion shows means bringing the runway into the viewers' living rooms. Users can experience the runway shows in real time from anywhere around the globe with just the need of a VR headset. They can see the models up close, watch the fabric detailings, and even move around the virtual space for different vantage points, creating a unique, immersive, and personalized runway experience.

6.4. Seeing Beyond 3D Models: Humanized Virtual Models

While the use of 3D designs, environments, and elements have significantly redefined the runway experience, the next step in the evolution – humanized virtual models – is set to take it a notch higher. Virtual models, also known as digital models or avatars, have the potential to offer a more realistic and dynamic runway experience. They can mimic actual human movements, break away from standard body dimensions, and offer endless customization possibilities, adding a new layer of resonance to the shows.

Big brands like Balmain and Gucci have already invested in creating their virtual models, signaling a future where digital and physical runways are set to exist symbiotically.

6.5. Digital Showrooms: Redefining Retail Experiences

An essential ripple effect of virtual fashion shows is the emergence of digital showrooms. These offer an extension of the immersive experience, allowing consumers to virtually try on the clothes they have just seen on the runway, providing them with a hands-on feel of the products. The extent of realism these tools can offer is remarkable and can lead to better purchase decisions as users can gauge how a garment would look and fit on their virtual avatar.

6.6. The Sustainability Impact: A Greener Future

One of the significant advantages of the shift towards virtual fashion shows is the positive impact on the environment. Traditional runway shows cost a fortune to put into action and have high carbon footprints— from production to set building to international travel. In contrast, virtual runways offer a dramatically more sustainable alternative, cutting down these costs and the carbon footprint significantly.

6.7. Forward in Fashion: The Future of Runways

The influence of virtual reality in fashion shows is profound and irreversible. Merging of the virtual runway with digital innovation leads us to a reality where fashion shows are more inclusive, sustainable, and engaging. More importantly, it brings along a sense of urgency for us, as an industry and as consumers, to embrace this transformation and be an active participant in redefining the future of fashion.

This is not only the future we are anticipating—it is the reality we are living. Not only does it promise progress but also ushers in a new era wherein fashion, technology, innovation, and creativity cross paths, creating a seamless, engaging, and sustainable future for the industry.

This is the runway revolution—the advent of virtual fashion shows delivering dazzling experiences right into our digital screens, pushing the creative boundaries of what a 'show' can be. The traditional catwalk is being reimagined and reinvented in ways that transcend geography, level the playing field, and offer a distinct mix of the physical and digital worlds—setting the stage for a truly revolutionary future ensconced in the realm of virtual reality.

Chapter 7. Tailored Experiences: Personalizing Style in Virtual Reality

In a world where personalisation is a key trend in almost every industry, VR technology has offered the fashion scene a new paradigm of possibilities. Virtual reality is no longer limited to realms of gaming or heavy-duty tech applications; instead, it breathes life into the creative spaces of haute couture and low-key fashion streetwear, gifting consumers with the ability to personalize their styles like never before.

7.1. Harnessing Personalization through VR

The power of personalization lies in its ability to celebrate individuality and uniqueness. No two individuals have the same taste in fashion, and VR technology's immersive nature allows fashion lovers to express and embrace their distinct style.

Through harnessing the power of VR, fashion labels can now immerse their consumers in an ultimate personalization journey—providing an avenue for individuals to customize their clothing in a 3D digital environment. Users can adjust colors, fabrics, sizes, patterns, and even the cut of a garment. The designs can be inspected from all angles, providing a comprehensive visualization of the end product.

7.2. Shaping Style: VR Fittings

Fittings have been a crucial part of the tailoring process for centuries, enabling the creation of garments that fit like a glove. VR technology takes this process to another level, simplifying and enriching fittings through digital avatars.

With the use of body-scanning technology, VR creates an accurate 3D model of the user. This digital model or avatar can be used to try on various designs, allowing users to see how individual garments look and identify needed alterations. While this process cannot entirely replace physical fittings, it provides initial drafts and ideas that users and tailors can work on, minimizing the number of physical fittings required.

7.3. Breaking Boundaries: Immersive Shopping Experiences

Beyond personalizing style, VR also reshapes retail experiences. Consumers can walk through virtual stores from the comforts of home, interacting with products as they would in a physical store—holding, trying, and even feeling the fabrics. This complete immersion breaks the barriers set by the traditional online shopping environment, transforming it into a more tactile and sensory experience that reflects the in-store shopping journey.

Furthermore, technological advancements like haptic feedback—the technology providing physical sensations to users—are being integrated with VR, offering unprecedented realistic experiences. This engages more senses, thus offering a more comprehensive understanding of products.

7.4. Fashion Accessibility: Bringing Runway Fashion to Your Living Room

VR brings the glitz of high-end fashion shows from cities like Paris and Milan right into people's living rooms. Users don VR headsets and are immediately transported to front row seats of virtual reality fashion shows. These experiences are not confined to showcasing fashion collections; users can also 'try on' garments and accessories presented on the catwalk. This interactive approach helps to bridge the gap between high-end fashion and the average consumer, proposing an accessible and democratic approach to fashion.

7.5. New Depths of Customer Data

VR applications can also collect and analyze comprehensive user data, such as accurate body measurements and preferences in style, color, and fabric. This data can be used by fashion brands to create highly personalized experiences for their customers, from tailor-made clothing to personalized shopping experiences. It also allows brands to identify emerging trends and make strategic decisions, thus making the fashion industry more customer-centric and data-driven.

7.6. Ethical Considerations

Although VR personalization fosters a new level of engagement in fashion, it does pose ethical challenges. The extensive data collection involves privacy risks, and there's a need to ensure these are managed properly. Effective data handling policies, transparency in data usage, and stringent cybersecurity measures are essential to maintaining user trust and ensuring their privacy is protected.

With VR technology's immersive capabilities and the era of hyper-personalization at the cusp, the fashion industry steps into a promising future where exquisite designs are not merely admired but lived. Everyone with an eye for style, tech enthusiasts, and casual fashion lovers alike, can engage with their unique style statement and craft their fashion narrative through virtual reality. While this integration of technology and fashion might seem daunting for some, remember that at its core, it's about celebrating individual expression. It's about personalizing fashion, making it more than a statement - making it an experience.

In the years to come, with VR becoming more affordable and sophisticated, we can expect the boundaries of this personalization to expand, providing increasing opportunities for consumers to shape their style and the industry's direction. Thus, riding firm on the belief that personalization is the ultimate form of luxury, VR endeavors to redefine style in its way, promising an unparalleled sartorial journey to every single one of its users.

Chapter 8. The Environmental Footprint: Sustainability and VR

The dialogue around fashion has grown louder over recent decades, driven by a broader awareness of climate change, pollution, and the importance of sustainable practices. With the rise of the digital era, Virtual Reality (VR) offers innovative ways to tackle the environmental footprint of the fashion industry. From conceptualization to production and retail, VR holds an array of opportunities to make the fashion industry greener.

8.1. The Fashion Industry's Carbon Footprint and The VR Solution

Historically, the fashion industry has had a high carbon footprint, owing to excessive production, material waste and the energy intensiveness of garment manufacturing. Recently, VR has started reshaping these conventional practices. Instead of producing physical prototypes, designers and brands can create virtual prototypes using VR. These models can be tweaked and perfected before a single physical sample is produced. This eliminates the time, resources, and waste associated with the traditional process, significantly mitigating the industry's carbon footprint.

8.2. Reimagining Material Sourcing Through VR

Another area that contributes heavily to the environmental footprint of the fashion industry's is raw material sourcing. Conventional fashion's reliance on non-renewable resources, transportation and production processes wreak havoc on global ecosystems. VR provides a solution through innovative methods like digital fabric sourcing. Designers can 'touch' and 'feel' the texture of textiles without the necessity to ship physical samples, reducing carbon emissions and revolutionizing the concept of sustainability in fashion.

8.3. The Future of Shopping: Eco-Friendly VR Stores

The transformation continues to retail experiences as well, seamlessly merging VR and sustainability. Traditional "brick and mortar" stores consume significant resources - from architecture to energy costs. A shift towards VR platforms reduces the resources necessary to create and maintain physical spaces.

Shoppers can enter immersive VR stores, regardless of geographic barriers, creating a new paradigm in retail. Consumers explore garments in hyper-realistic 3D digital showrooms, enjoying enhanced user experiences, and directly contributing to less carbon emissions and environmental degradation.

8.4. Digital Runways and Sustainable Shows

Fashion weeks and runway shows have been the cornerstone of high fashion. However, their environmental impact is massive, from the global travel of attendees to the physical infrastructure setup. Virtual Reality offers a sustainable alternative to these traditional modes.

Designers are now adopting VR-powered fashion shows, where their collection can be showcased in a virtual environment. Attendees simply wear a VR headset and immerse themselves in the designer's creative space, saving a significant amount of energy and resources. Virtual Reality has democratized the fashion show experience, making it more accessible and drastically more sustainable.

8.5. Tech-Powered Ethics: Influence on Consumer Behavior

VR can also play a significant role in the ethical side of sustainability, particularly in helping consumers make more informed and responsible purchases. Through interactive VR documentaries and exposés, brands can give consumers an immersive look into their supply chains, production processes, and commitment to sustainability. This transparency can inspire consumers to reevaluate their purchasing habits, fostering a more sustainable and conscious global fashion industry.

8.6. Final Thoughts: A Greener Future with VR

While Virtual Reality is still a nascent technology in the world of fashion, its implications for sustainability are vast and promising. As consumers become more environmentally conscious and technology advances, the fusion of VR with fashion will create significant positive impacts. Striving towards more responsible creative processes, better carbon footprints, and a more accountable industry, VR opens the door to a future where fashion doesn't compromise the health of our planet.

This journey into a greener fashion industry isn't just about adopting VR technology; it's about revamping our ideologies and valuing sustainability as much as style. As we continue to navigate through this digital evolution, there is more than ever to gain by embracing this confluence of technology and fashion with open minds. After all, the future of fashion is not just about what we wear, but how we create, experience, and impact the world around us.

Chapter 9. Virtual Reality's Impact on Fashion Education

The transformation ignited by Virtual Reality technologies in various sectors is truly magnificent, and the realm of fashion education is not an exception. VR has opened doors to endless possibilities and education in fashion is swiftly embracing this trend.

9.1. Introduction to VR in Fashion Education

As a nascent-yet-potent tool, VR is reimagining boundaries in fashion education. The traditional classrooms are now fitted with VR headsets, paving the way for enthralling and engaging ways of learning. Teachers and students can visualize, model, and interact with fashion designs and models using a 360-degree perspective, shattering the vicinity constraints of a traditional classroom.

9.2. Understanding the Fashion Design Process

Comprehending the intricacies of fashion design is an integral part of fashion education. VR enables students to closely observe and interact with each stage of the design process. They can view the raw design, experiment with different textile materials, colors and see the impact of those changes real-time. This virtual experimentation saves physical resources and allows students to learn from their mistakes without significant repercussions.

9.3. 3D Designing Tools

Three-dimensional design tools are a natural evolution in art and design education. Virtual spaces give fashion students a boundary to craft their designs, explore shapes, silhouettes, and textures, and virtually drape them onto virtual mannequins. These VR-based tools not only save time and cost of material but they also reduce the margin for error, making the learning process more efficient.

9.4. Virtual Workshops and Labs

VR offers an interactive platform for workshops and labs that can be accessed from any corner of the world. Lending a true-to-life experience, these VR labs can simulate realistic situations such as fashion shows, manufacturing units, store setups, and much more. Learners can partake in these virtual simulations to understand the behind-the-scenes work without actually being physically present.

9.5. Real-world Simulation

Education is the backbone of preparedness for real-world challenges. A paramount advantage of VR is its ability to simulate real-world difficulties and customer reactions to design choices. It prepares learners for the fashion industry's impromptu challenges through an accurate knowledge experience, and nurtures their skills in adapting swiftly to the continuously evolving digital world.

9.6. Sustainability and Ethical Fashion

The world is becoming environmentally-conscious, which leads to an increasing emphasis on sustainability and ethical fashion. Virtual Reality serves as an excellent tool to educate future designers about these concepts, allowing them to simulate different manufacturing processes, material uses, and observe the impacts on the environment in a controlled setting.

9.7. Collaboration and Team Projects

One of the key learning pathways in fashion education is collaboration. Virtual Reality aids in fostering collaboration by creating shared virtual environments where students, irrespective of their geographical location, can work together on projects, share ideas, and innovate collectively.

9.8. Building the Virtual Portfolios

The fashion industry requires demonstrating creativity and talent visually. Now, students can take advantage of VR technology to create impressive virtual portfolios, showcasing their work in 3D or even in simulations of real-life scenarios.

9.9. Enhancing the Retail Experience

VR in fashion education is not restricted to design and manufacturing; it permeates the retail experiences as well. Understanding the nuances of retail is crucial for any fashion student. VR can simulate busy stores or luxurious spaces for learners to understand customer behavior, marketing strategies, and make them competent enough to tackle real-world scenarios.

Teachers should acquaint themselves with this futuristic tool to craft an all-inclusive curriculum that represents how the fashion industry is being reshaped. The future fashion leaders should not only be adept at creating beautiful designs, but they should also be versatile, tech-savant strategists who can effectively use technology to their advantage.

Despite the sophistication and prowess of VR, challenges remain around widespread adoption. Concerns about cost, adaptability, and the potential for alienation in a VR environment must be addressed. Yet, the promise of what VR can deliver for fashion education, from enhanced design visualizations, better presentations, and improved collaborative spaces, appears well worth confronting these obstacles.

In summary, the introduction of VR in fashion education is revolutionizing the traditional modes of learning, introducing larger-than-life experiences and opening a new world of opportunities. It is redefining how knowledge is captured, and skills are honed to prepare this generation to be future-ready and the next to be visionaries. As we continue to evolve with this fast-paced digital world, the future of fashion education glistens brightly!

Chapter 10. Social Reality: VR and the Future of Fashion Marketing

We live in an era where technology continuously blurs the lines between reality and digital representations, opening a new world for us to explore and interact with. Virtual Reality (VR), with its ability to create immersive virtual environments, stands at the heart of this digital revolution. The fashion industry, constantly in search of innovative marketing tactics and more engaging narratives, is increasingly adopting this technological marvel to shape the future of fashion marketing.

10.1. VR: The Marketing Marvel

Advancements in VR technology enabled brands to provide an immersive shopping experience that has significant advantages over the traditional way. Imagine going through a fashion catalog, but instead of just visually engaging with 2D representations, you have the opportunity to enter an immersive world, try clothes on your virtual avatar, and experience a real-life fashion show from the comfort of your home. This type of interactivity offered by VR not only enhances customer engagement but also propels a more personalized brand-consumer relationship.

Moreover, VR also creates an environment where buyers can virtually "meet" with designers to discuss their preferences, creating a sense of exclusivity usually reserved for high-end customers. By merging the boundaries of physical and digital, VR throws open a door to endless possibilities, changing the traditional consumer-brand dynamics.

10.2. Rewriting Retail: Virtual Showrooms

The charm of VR goes beyond just virtual fitting rooms. The concept of virtual showrooms offers a new dimension in delivering unrivaled retail experiences. Be it high-street fashion brands or bespoke luxury houses – everyone can now facilitate their customers to scale every product detail in 3D, revamp their wardrobes virtually or visualize themselves at exotic locations, all from storefronts that can change with the click of a button.

The particularly exciting aspect of virtual showrooms is the elimination of geographical barriers. Shoppers across the globe can now access the latest designs, irrespective of where they live. Thus, brands can tap into a larger audience, even those in remote locations, escalating their global reach.

10.3. Catwalks and Collections: VR Fashion Shows

Traditionally, fashion shows are events witnessed by an exclusive few, unless you consider the people streaming it on various platforms. However, VR offers front-row seats to everyone interested, directly from their living room. For instance, the virtual show by Balenciaga in 2020 was a revolutionizing moment in the fashion industry. Their dystopian video game format allowed the audience to engage and control the interactions with the collection, leading to a one-of-a-kind user experience.

Such shows make for an immersive narrative, and they redefine fashion marketing strategies. An excellent instance of marrying storytelling with consumer interest, VR fashion shows bring the runway to the audience in an unprecedented manner.

10.4. Tailoring A Sustainable Future

Innovative marketing is not the only advantage of VR technology. It also has a crucial role in promoting sustainability in the fashion industry. As VR negates the need for physical samples and prototypes, it aids in reducing waste production significantly. Fashion brands can now create design prototypes virtually and only proceed to manufacturing after final approval, thus minimizing textile waste.

Moreover, as VR allows remote access to showrooms and fashion shows, it reduces travel, thereby lowering carbon footprint. In an era where consumers are increasingly environmentally conscious, VR becomes an asset, presenting a novel way to balance innovation with sustainability.

10.5. Immersive Storytelling: Striking a Deeper Connection

A particularly exciting consequence of VR in fashion marketing lies in its ability to deliver immersive storytelling. The fashion world thrives on narratives that elicit emotional responses and associations with the brand. VR acts as an ideal platform for this purpose. Unlike traditional mediums, VR allows the user to be physically present in the story, thus forming a deeper connection. It transitions the user from a mere spectator to an active participant, capitalizing on experiential marketing and forming deeper bonds with consumers.

Taking everything into account, VR boldly revolutionizes traditional dynamics, marking the dawn of a new era in fashion marketing. It surpasses geographical barriers, creates a personalized shopping experience, brings the exclusivity of fashion shows to everyone, and opens avenues for sustainable practices. Witnessing the trajectory VR is on, we are on the brink of experiencing a seismic shift in the fashion industry. One where boundaries of the physical world cease to exist, and a virtual world that is as engaging, immersive, and exciting awaits us.

VR and the future of fashion marketing are entwined in such a manner that isolating one from the other might soon become impossibility. As technology continues to advance at an accelerated pace, the involvement of VR in fashion marketing will likely deepen, making it an integral part of the industry. Perhaps, the question we should be asking is not if, but how transformative VR's impact on the fashion industry will be in the coming years.

Chapter 11. The Path Forward: Challenges and Prospects of VR in Fashion

The journey into Virtual Reality's impact on the fashion industry begins with a simple but profound idea: a world where garments are designed, showcased, and experienced in three-dimensional spaces, unhindered by physical boundaries or constraints. As we delve deeper into this concept, we encounter both excitement and apprehension regarding its potential. The key elements shaping the future of VR in the fashion industry are its challenges, issues to be resolved, and prospects that invite exploration and experimentation.

11.1. The Challenges Facing VR in Fashion

Despite its immense potential, the implementation of VR in fashion is not without challenges. A closer look unveils a plethora of issues that need addressing for seamless integration into the fashion industry.

Firstly, the technology itself requires significant improvements. Despite the advancement of VR headsets and their increasing affordability, there are still issues with user comfort, image quality, and motion sickness. These barriers significantly affect the user experience, directly impacting the way fashion enthusiasts view and experience the virtual designs and retail spaces.

Secondly, from the viewpoint of brands and designers, VR technology requires substantial investment in terms of time and money. High-quality VR experiences necessitate intricate 3D modeling, meticulous design, and seamless rendering, all time-consuming and costly processes.

Furthermore, integrating VR into the typical purchase journey can be complex. While some brands have successfully done this—such as Tommy Hilfiger, which offered a virtual reality view of its runway shows in select stores around the world—this approach is not yet widely adopted. Buyers, whether individuals or retail buyers for stores, might remain skeptical about using VR as part of their buying process risk-averse given that the technology still feels relatively new.

Lastly, the educational gap is a significant, yet often overlooked challenge. For the industry to fully embrace VR, fashion students need to learn how to design in 3D and use VR tools, a skill set not typically taught in most fashion institutes.

11.2. The Prospects of VR in Fashion

While the challenges of integrating VR into the fashion industry are numerous, they are not insurmountable. The industry's future with VR holds tremendous potential that extends beyond being a mere sales or marketing tool.

VR could revolutionize the creative process within fashion design. With VR, designers would be able to manipulate their designs in a three-dimensional space, providing them with a better perspective of their work. They could experiment with the drape of a fabric, adjust the shape and structure of garments, and explore different styles with ease—all contributing to a more creative and efficient design process that benefits not only the designers but also the consumers who wear their creations.

Another exciting prospect is the transformative power of VR for fashion shows and retail experiences. Envision a world where consumers could attend virtual fashion shows, immersing themselves fully in the styled atmosphere created by the brands—taking a front-row seat at some of the most exclusive events in the fashion calendar. With VR, shopping could become a much more immersive experience that doesn't require physical presence—a life-size experience right in the comfort of one's home, with the world's best boutiques just a click away.

Amid growing concerns for sustainability, VR holds a promising solution. Virtual clothing could decrease overproduction, a major source of waste in the industry. Buyers could fit clothes on their virtual avatars before making a purchase, thereby reducing the rate of returns—a solid step towards a more sustainable industry.

Moreover, Virtual Reality could democratize the fashion industry, taking high fashion from a traditionally exclusive domain to one where everyone has front-row access. With more people involved, the industry would become more diverse and potentially more innovative.

11.3. Charting The Path Forward

The path forward for VR in fashion promises to be intriguing, as the technology holds enormous potential for transformation. As with any burgeoning technology, the challenges are present, but so too are exciting possibilities and benefits.

To truly tap into VR's potential, it's essential that industry stakeholders—technologists, designers, retailers, educators, and consumers all come together to address the challenges and explore the prospects. Collaboration would be crucial to shape the future, and in doing so, it's vital that we keep inclusivity, creativity, and sustainability at the forefront.

The road towards melding VR into the fashion industry is a progressive one filled with constant advancement and development. The key to success lies in perseverance, collaboration, and the willingness to continuously learn, test, and innovate.

In conclusion, the acquisition of comprehensive knowledge

regarding VR's implementation in fashion, including its challenges and prospects, deepens our understanding as we venture into this technological frontier. As we paint the canvas of the fashion industry with the colors of Virtual Reality, each brushstroke represents an intricate weave of creativity, technology, and our vision of a remarkable, fashionable future.

As we progress, innovation continues to redefine tradition—unfolding a vibrant, ever-evolving universe in fashion. Our journey is just beginning, and the best is probably yet to come. So, let's step forward together into the future, where the fabric of reality reshapes itself endlessly under the spell of our imagination.